fanciest courtship / best mimic

smelliest

WITHDRAWN

longest bill

most gruesome prey collection

longest round-trip migration

widest field of view

keenest sense of smell

biggest nest

most brilliantly colored eggs

Superlative Birds

Superlative
Birds

Written by **Leslie Bulion**

Illustrated by **Robert Meganck**

PEACHTREE
ATLANTA

For Jerry Theise and his beloved birds
—L. B.

To my wife, Candace, who has installed so many bird feeders in our yard
that I frequently refer to it as "a good setting for a Hitchcock movie"
—R. M.

Published by
PEACHTREE PUBLISHERS
1700 Chattahoochee Avenue
Atlanta, Georgia 30318-2112
www.peachtree-online.com

Text © 2019 by Leslie Bulion
Illustrations © 2019 by Robert Meganck

Edited by Vicky Holifield
Design and composition by Robert Meganck
Art direction by Nicola Simmonds Carmack

The illustrations were rendered digitally.

For information about the voice artist singing "Arctic Terns the World 'Round," visit *www.juliahirsch.com.*

Printed in August 2018 by Tien Wah, Malaysia
10 9 8 7 6 5 4 3 2 1
First Edition

ISBN 978-1-56145-951-3

Library of Congress Cataloging-in-Publication Data

Names: Bulion, Leslie, 1958– author. | Meganck, Robert, illustrator.
Title: Superlative birds / written by Leslie Bulion ; illustrated by Robert Meganck.
Description: First edition. | Atlanta : Peachtree Publishers, [2019] | Audience: Age 8–12. | Audience: Grade 4 to 6. | Includes bibliographical references.
Identifiers: LCCN 2018000343 | ISBN 9781561459513
Subjects: LCSH: Birds—Miscellanea—Juvenile literature.
Classification: LCC QL676.2 .B83 2019 | DDC 598—dc23 LC record available at *https://lccn.loc.gov/2018000343*

CONTENTS

Superlative Birds

Which birds can do what birds do, *best*?
Which put world records to the test?
Which birds are beaks above the rest?
Superlative birds! Come see!

Which birdly traits leave us impressed?
The longest toes? The largest nest?
Most feathers for the warmest dressed?
Let's read on and see...

Who's smallest? Who's the fastest flier?
Deepest diver? Loudest crier?
Stores most dead prey on barbed wire?
This we've got to see!

But...
Which traits give birds special flair,
On land, at sea, and in the air,
Traits only birds (and *most* birds) share?
Do you know? Let's see!

Pssst—
if you need
a birdbrain hint,
ask me...
the chickadee!

Less Than a Penny

Wingbeats blur
whirrrr
too swift to see.
A glimmer—
shiny
tiny
barely bigger
than a bee—
sips nectar,
buzzzzzing
flower to flower,
using
figure-eight
hovercraft
hummer power.

Even this tiny hummer has those special traits belonging only to birds. Think you know what those traits are? Follow me!

Science Note

The bee hummingbird (*Mellisuga helenae*) is the **smallest** bird in the world. Found only on the Caribbean island nation of Cuba, this hummingbird is about as long as a baby carrot and weighs less than a penny. You would need eighty thousand bee hummingbirds to balance a seesaw with the world's biggest bird, the 344-pound (156-kilogram) ostrich! The bee hummingbird must sip lots of nectar and eat plenty of insect fuel to power its busy wings, which beat in a figure-eight pattern more than eighty times per second.

Sunlight catches the structure of certain bird feathers—like those on the male bee hummingbird's head and throat—to make shimmering, iridescent colors. Most of the blues or greens we see on bird feathers are also due to the way light strikes the distinctive structure of those feathers. Black and brown feathers get their hue from melanin, a chemical made by birds' bodies. Red, yellow, and orange feather colors come from substances in the foods birds eat.

A Billion Queleas

Red-billed queleas wheeling, nesting,
Dawn brings wild seed feast, then resting,
Dry season's end sends queleas pesting,
Seeking fields of crop-grown grasses.

Still air fills with *chee-chee* chattering,
Farmer CLANGS a noisy CLATTERing,
Queleas billow, rising, scattering,
Seeking wild savannah grasses.

> Many birds flock, but not all do. Sheep flock and other animals gather in groups, too!

Science Note

South of the Sahara Desert in Africa, great clouds of sparrow-sized red-billed queleas (KWEE-lee-uhs) rise and fall, sipping at waterholes, settling on branches, and clinging to stalks of wild grasses. The red-billed quelea (*Quelea quelea*) is the **most numerous** living bird on Earth with an estimated adult population of 1.5 billion birds. Though a single quelea weighs less than one ounce (28 grams), huge flocks containing millions of birds can collapse a tree when they land for a nighttime roost!

Scientists think that birds flock to share information about food sources and to lessen the chance they'll be picked off by a predator. Flocking may also give birds lots of choices for a mate. Emperor penguins flock to share warmth. Geese flying in a V formation save energy in flight.

At the end of the dry season, when wild grass seed grows scarce, quelea flocks become farm pests, stripping seeds from planted grasses like wheat, millet, and rice. Farmers often make noise to scare these seed thieves away.

The Flying Leap

Built
to swim
not too slim
we don't fly
wouldn't try
waddle stop
belly-flop, slip
slide toboggan
glide—icy dash ends
with SPLASH! Wings
are fins for twirls and
spins, we plunge below
pack ice and snow for
fish for krill for squid until
we've fished our fill. Our
young ones will be overjoyed
if we avoid becoming meals
for leopard seals lurking grim
at ice floe's rim. We know they're there
we're well aware so we prepare: our feathers trap air.
When we release bubbles our
swimming speed DOUBLES!
We jet from the sea
predator-free
we catch air—*wheeeee!*

Eureka! We found a special trait that belongs only to birds, and all birds have them—feathers!

Science Note

Research suggests that the emperor penguin (*Aptenodytes forsteri*) in Antarctica has the **most feathers** of any bird studied so far. The largest emperor penguins were estimated to have more than thirty thousand contour feathers on their bodies alone. Contour feathers are stiff outer feathers that protect a bird and give it shape. Shorter, downy, plume-shaped feathers help keep birds warm.

Birds use special oils produced by their bodies to preen (clean, straighten, and zip together) their feathers, most often by pulling feathers through their bills. This regular conditioning helps the emperor penguin's feathers protect it from icy Antarctic air and water.

Preening also helps the emperor penguin in another way. Just before returning from a fishing trip, the penguin surfaces to preen, trapping air in its downy feather layer. Then it dives again, releasing its trapped air to form a tunnel of tiny underwater bubbles. (This bird is the **deepest diver**, too!) The bubbles help the penguin slip through water at more than double its swimming speed so it can rocket ashore past hungry leopard seals waiting at the edge of the ice. Nice!

Walk On Water

The jacana splays spindly toes,
Skip-trots across broad lily pads,
Picks tasty insects as it goes.

Young jacanas kept warm by Dad,
Tuck under wing, with trailing toes
too long to fit, but still—not bad!

How long are your toes?

Science Note

The northern jacana (*Jacana spinosa*) is a marsh bird from Mexico, Central America, and South America. Like most birds, the jacana (zha-sah-NAH) has four toes. Many birds share the jacana's arrangement of three toes pointing forward and one backward. Tree-climbing birds usually have two toes forward and two backward. Relative to its small-ish body size, the jacana has the **longest toes** of any bird—three inches (7.6 centimeters) long!

When it splays those four skinny toes, the jacana's body weight of 1/4 pound (113 grams) is distributed across a wide area so it can walk on floating lily pads without sinking. Large flightless birds like ostriches, emus, and cassowaries have toes longer than three inches. Still, the emu's five-inch (12.7-centimeter) toes can't spread its whopping 99 pounds (45 kilograms) of body weight out far enough for it to walk on a lily pad.

The Wanderer

Who knows where the albatross goes,
Skimming seas where Antarctic wind blows?
It quits land a young thing,
For lone years on the wing,
While it leaks salty tears from its nose.

Who knows how the albatross goes,
While soaring through sunburst and snows?
Their wingspan's so wide,
They don't flap much, they glide,
And may shut half their brain if they doze.

All birds have wings. But other animals have wings, too!

Science Note

The long, narrow wings of the wandering albatross are built to soar on the blustery winds of the Antarctic Ocean. Measuring nearly 12 feet (3.7 meters) from wingtip to wingtip, the wandering albatross (*Diomedea exulans*) has the **widest wingspan** of all birds. Albatross wings lock in place at the "elbows," allowing this oceanic bird to sail upward into a cross-breeze then glide far ahead as gravity pulls it seaward once again.

After it fledges (leaves the nest), a wandering albatross flies over the sea to forage for fish and squid. It won't return to land until it's ready to mate in five to seven years, but it can float on the ocean for a few hours at night. The albatross is a "tubenose"—a type of seabird that can drink seawater and expel salt through tubes on its bill.

Some species of birds can close one eye and power down half their brain. They may even do so while flying. Does the albatross soar too close to the water to snooze-fly? Ornithologists (bird scientists) are studying birds' sleep patterns to find out.

Bird Hunter

wings trim
peregrine knifes earthward
from sky scraper cliff
bold spirit embodies
the shape of speed

Bird
Skeleton

keel

Wish you had this bone?
Sorry! The furcula is the
second trait found only
in birds!

Science Note

The peregrine falcon (*Falco peregrinus*) is a medium-sized raptor found on many oceanic islands and every continent except Antarctica. With wings tucked in a streamlined dive known as a stoop, the peregrine has clocked in at 242 miles (390 kilometers) per hour, which makes it the **fastest** creature on Earth. The peregrine dives from heights of up to 3000 feet (914 meters) to stun smaller prey birds with a strike from its sharp talons.

The breastbone of flying birds stretches forward from the ribs into a flat blade called the keel. A bird's flight muscles attach on either side of the keel. In the peregrine, the keel is very wide, allowing plenty of room to anchor the large flight muscles that power this bird's pointy wings.

The furcula, a strong, flexible bone found only in birds, gives extra support to a bird's shoulders. The furcula bends in and out as wings flap and move. *Most* birds—including birds that don't fly—have this bone in their skeleton, too. You may have seen a furcula—it's the wishbone in a cooked chicken or turkey.

Paleontologists have learned that many dinosaurs had feathers, a furcula, or both—two of the strong evolutionary links supporting the view that birds are living dinosaurs!

Science Note

The Arctic tern (*Sterna paradisaea*) is a smallish sea bird with the **longest round-trip migration** recorded for any animal on Earth: a whopping 50,703 miles (81,600 kilometers) from the Antarctic to the Arctic and back again!

When Earth's northern hemisphere tilts toward the sun in summer, colonies of Arctic terns nest on the ground along the northernmost Arctic Ocean shores worldwide. There, terns enjoy a rich summer food supply and nearly twenty-four hours of daylight as they fish for the energy they need to lay eggs and feed chicks.

As oncoming winter brings increasing darkness to the Arctic, terns take to the air. From August to November, Arctic terns migrate southward over open ocean and along continental coasts, following the southern hemisphere's tilt toward *its* long hours of summer daylight. Among the Antarctic ice floes, terns find plenty of fish and krill to refuel for the long spring flight back to their Arctic breeding grounds.

Arctic Terns the World 'Round

Night falls, each day's length is shrinking,
The evening sun sinks as the summer slips by,
Light calls, terns take to wing, linking
Earth's Arctic and Antarctic summer-bright sky.

Tern wings, built long, sharp, and narrow,
Will carry and lift terns on wind as they soar
Southbound, but not straight as an arrow,
Terns tarry and fish at sites distant from shore.

Yo-ho! Arctic terns go
Where prevailing winds blow!

Antarctic seas make a fine feeding station,
Terns fill up on krill, the supply is unmatched,
Summer fades, northward Arctic migration
Returns terns to breeding grounds where they once hatched.

Yo-ho! Arctic terns go
Where prevailing winds blow!

Night falls, each day's length is shrinking,
The evening sun sinks as the summer slips by,
Light calls, terns take to wing, linking
Earth's Arctic and Antarctic summer-bright sky.

Scan here and sing along!

All birds have bills, but so does the duck-billed platypus. And octopuses and turtles have beaks!

Crayfish for Supper

"My bill can feel prey underwater,"
the Australian pelican said.
"With the hook at its tip,
I grip fish, that I flip
down my throat with a jerk of my head."

"No worries," said the pelican,
"though I've a deep pouch to fill.
If I dipper for fish,
and they flee with a swish,
yummy yabbies fit the bill."

Science Note

The Australian pelican (*Pelecanus conspicillatus*) is a medium-sized pelican with the **longest bill** ever measured on a bird—nearly 20 inches (50 centimeters) long. Birds use their beaks (also called bills) for a variety of activities, including preening, performing courtship displays, building nests, foraging for food, and feeding young. Bill shapes match each bird's feeding style: short, finchy cones for cracking seeds; hooked, hawkish bills for tearing flesh; or the long, nectar-sipping straws of hummingbirds.

The Australian pelican uses its long bill and stretchy throat pouch to herd, grab, and scoop favorite prey such as carp or perch. Pressing its throat pouch against its chest, the pelican squeezes out water and jerks its head upward to reposition its catch before swallowing. Inside the Australian pelican's long bill, its relatively small tongue stays far in the back near its throat to tighten its pouch and to help force down food such as crabs, small reptiles, common yabbies (a freshwater crayfish), and, unfortunately, even human food waste from landfills.

The Ghastly Pantry

A most surprising songbird is the shrike.
Small scurriers had better stay away,
Or else they'll end up skewered on a pike.
A most surprising songbird is the shrike.
It darts down from its perch to make a strike,
Then decorates long thorns with rotting prey.
A most surprising songbird is the shrike—
Small scurriers had better stay away!

Many other animals store food, too. And lots of birds eat food as they find it!

Science Note

Shrikes perch on open branches, wires, and ledges in North America, Eurasia, and Africa. In the world of birds, these songbirds may be smallish predators, but they keep the **most gruesome prey collection** of any bird.

Most predatory birds eat prey when they kill it. They may bring portions back to the nest, or spit up partly digested tidbits for their chicks. Some birds—including predatory birds—hide extra food, especially when food is scarce.

When the northern shrike (*Lanius borealis*) spots live prey, it plummets swiftly, often killing its quarry with one beak jab to the neck. Then this "butcher bird" adorns a thorny tree or nearby barbed wire with its catch: dead rodents, small birds, reptiles, amphibians, or juicy insects. Hanging prey rots until it's soft enough for the shrike's small beak and claws to dig in. Delish!

reptiles

insects

fish

Birds aren't the only animals that lay interesting eggs!

Science Note

Eggs are elegant packages of protection and nutrition for developing chick embryos. The tinamou, a plump-bellied ground-nesting bird from the rainforests of Central and South America, lays the **most brilliantly colored eggs** of all birds. Each species of tinamou lays eggs in a glossy color such as iridescent green, dark purple, or even the shiny turquoise of the great tinamou (*Tinamus major*).

Unlike most birds, the tinamou male incubates the eggs. More than one hen may add her eggs to each male's nest. This strategy helps each hen since there's a chance that an egg grabbed from the nest by a predator might not be hers. But why don't tinamous lay eggs that match the forest floor as most ground-nesting birds do?

Do the streaky brown, camouflaged males sit on the nest scrape longer to hide those brightly colored eggs? Or do the fancy colors help males identify their eggs? Egg color fades with time and may signal to new tinamou hens that it's too late to add eggs to the clutch. Ornithologists who study tinamous have many good questions!

Iridescent Eggs

A nesting tinamou is found,
Not in a tree, but on the ground,
A round, drab bird with thick-boned legs,
Who sits on iridescent eggs.

Its soil-bed nest is called a scrape,
An unlined, shallow, bowl-ish shape,
Designed by hen with beak, not legs,
Who then lays iridescent eggs.

When eggs are in, she leaves the scene
To forage, mate again, or preen.
Who'll incubate? The question begs:
Who'll warm her iridescent eggs?

Once tinamou mom calls it quits,
A dad bird saunters in and sits,
He parks his rump and tucks his legs,
He claims those iridescent eggs.

When hungry dad darts out for food,
A *new* hen sneaks up (that seems rude),
She scuttles in on stealthy legs,
And adds *her* iridescent eggs.

On glossy eggs from careless clucks,
Are rooster dads just sitting ducks?
They're camouflaged from beak to legs—
Why sit on iridescent eggs?

Timberdoodle Blues

Look at me, I've got eyes set up above my brain,
Not behind, on the sides—but *above* my brain,
Looks weird, but I see three-sixty and can't complain.

I can look up and back without moving my head,
Just like I've got eyes in back of my head,
I've got my eye on you from my leaf litter bed.

My buffy brown splotches camouflage me so well,
Mottled flecks and splotches hide me so well,
I can keep my eye on you and you can't even tell.

My bill's shaped long and straight to hunt worms in the mud,
I probe and poke, hunting worms in the mud,
My bill's down, but I've still got my eye on you, bud.

Unlike the timberdoodle, most birds can't see in a full 360-degree circle. But dragonflies and chameleons can!

Science Note

The American woodcock (*Scolopax minor*) is a short-legged shorebird found in moist forests of eastern North America. While most birds have eyes set on the sides of their heads, the American woodcock, nicknamed "timberdoodle," has eyes on top of its head. This gives it the **widest field of view** of all birds. Though many raptors are known to have keen eyesight, only the woodcock can see in a full circle without moving.

With its camouflaged feathers and no need to turn or tip its head, the plump little timberdoodle can keep an eye out everywhere without making movements predators might spot.

After dark, timberdoodles emerge from cover to probe soil and mud with their long, straight bills. Their top-set eyes also allow them to see all the way up and down, so timberdoodles can scan for hungry great horned owls overhead *and* poke for earthworms at the same time—a lifesaving talent for this slow-flying bird!

Calling Contest

If you visit
the rainforest in Central America
and you are very lucky
you might be near enough
to hear
BONNNK!
BONNNK!
SQUEEEE!
the woggling ping
of the three-wattled bellbird:
Here I am!
I make the biggest sound of all!
But if you are too close
this jackhammer call
pounds your eardrums.

If you visit
the island of Seram in Indonesia
and you are very very lucky
you might be near enough
to hear
EH-EH-EH-EH-EH!
RRRAAAAAAK!
PIKAAAAW!
the salmon-crested cockatoo's
jungle shout-out:
Here I am!
I make the biggest sound of all!

But if you are too close
this chainsaw call
RATTLES your eardrums.

If you visit
a night forest in New Zealand
and you are very, very, very lucky
you might hear
BOOOOM!
BOOOOM!
BOOOOM!
the deep rumble rising
from an earthbound bowl
kicked smooth by the kakapo:
Here I am!
I make the biggest sound of all!
This foghorn call
thrum-m-m-ms your eardrums
even
if
you
are

  very

    very

      very

        far
          away.

Science Note

Birds *call* to send out alerts and to communicate with their flocks or chicks. Birds *sing* to defend territories, attract mates, and sometimes to bond with mates in singing duets. Their songs and calls are produced with a two-sided voice organ called the syrinx. The most spectacular bird sounds are nearly always made by male birds.

Ornithologists think a male three-wattled bellbird (*Procnias tricarunculatus*) singing his heart out in a South American rainforest may be signaling to females that he's strong enough to defend the best territory. The salmon-crested cockatoo (*Cacatua moluccensis*) from Indonesia may use his high-pitched squawks to convince cockatoo hens he's healthy and fit. New Zealand's kakapo (*Strigops habroptila*) inflates its throat to belch deep, bone-rattling advertisements that travel for miles through the forest understory.

To compare sound levels (measured in decibels) these noisemakers would have to be the same distance from the recording device. So it's difficult to say for certain which of these birds is the **BIGGEST loudmouth**!

Barn Owl Papa

Silent wings brush nighttime air,
Be wary, lemming, vole, and hare—
Owlets need their growing share.

Papa swoops, a downward shear,
Toward rustlings only barn owls hear;
He hunts by supersonic ear.

Some other night-hunting owls have uneven ears and extra-sharp hearing, but *most* birds don't.

Science Note

The barn owl (*Tyto alba*) has the **most accurate hearing** of any animal tested. This raptor hunts by night in forests, deserts, marshes, grasslands, suburbs, and cities on every continent except Antarctica. A soft fringe of feathers on the lower edge of the barn owl's wings muffles sound from its wingbeats as the owl dips from its perch to grab scurrying prey.

Stiff feathers called a ruff frame the sides of the barn owl's face, creating a bowl shape. When the barn owl turns its head toward a rodent's rustle, the ruff works like a satellite dish to collect and direct sound waves to an ear slit at each side. One ear opening is a bit higher than the other. This unequal placement allows sound waves to reach each of the owl's ears at slightly different times. This time difference helps the barn owl pinpoint the exact location of its prey without needing to see it at all!

33

Turkey Vulture

This vulture
stands
on chickeny feet
and doesn't tweet
or cluck
or peep
or cheep.
It hisses and grunts
and hunts
on the fly,
gliding
impossibly high
on thermals of air,
with its head scaly red
and wrinkly
and bare.
Its nose
knows aromas
from way up there,
of detectable
delectable
fare
to share,
so things dead
(or deader)
had better
beware!

Science Note

The turkey vulture (*Cathartes aura*) is a large raptor from North and South America that eats mostly carrion (the meat from dead animals). It has no syrinx and can't sing, but the turkey vulture has been shown to have the **keenest sense of smell** of any bird studied. Locating carrion from far away is a good skill for this meat-eating bird whose beak and talons are not strong enough to kill and carry prey.

Though the turkey vulture appears clumsy on the ground, it is graceful in flight. Holding its broad wings in a V, it uses rising warm air currents called thermals to soar and circle. It can't call out in flight, so instead, as a turkey vulture tracks odor cues to find carrion, it also keeps an eye on its fellow fliers. When one turkey vulture descends, the others follow and join in a deliciously dead group meal.

34

What's in a Hoatzin?

Blunt stub beak,
Bald blue cheek,
A scraggly, scrappy crest.

Fierce red eye,
Hiss-grunt cry,
Klutzy flight, at best.

All-day rest,
To perch, digest,
Crop full of leaves and blooms.

While food ferments,
Crop belches scents,
Like fine cow poo perfumes.

Hen feeds her brood
Mom-processed food,
(she barfs to feed each chick).

Grown birds *and* young
Then stink like dung—
A bird-world super trick!

Science Note

The hoatzin (WHAT-zin) lives in the Amazon and Orinoco Basins of South America. The hoatzin (*Opisthocomus hoazin*) has been called the **smelliest** bird in the world! Its digestion process smells so terrible that people don't hunt or eat it even though these birds are plentiful, slow, and about the size of a small goose.

Food passes quickly through the digestive system of birds that eat insects, seeds, and fruit. Food may be stored in an organ called the crop for a short time before it passes into the bird's two-part stomach where most of digestion happens.

But a hoatzin's diet of tough-to-digest leaves takes a LOT longer to process. The hoatzin perches near the water all day while microbes (microscopic organisms) and digestive juices in its crop and the lower, folded part of its esophagus (food tube) slo-o-owly break leaves down into usable nutrients. Microbes helping with digestion produce gas that smells like cow manure. *Buurrrp!*

Some birds don't have crops. But earthworms *do*.

CROP

Pick Me!

One superb young lyrebird scratched soil into a mound,
Under the shade of a tallow-wood tree,
Then he climbed on the mound and he called out to the lady birds,
"I'm here to wow you, come courting with me!"

"I'm here a-courting! I'm here a-courting!
Lyrebird ladies come flock around me!
I've the finest display on Australia's leafy forest floor.
You need my genes for your own family tree."

Next that saucy lyrebird fanned out his fancy tail,
He tipped it forward and shook it with glee,
"Look! Fancy feathers to impress you with my splendidness,
I'm here to wow you, come courting with me."

"Look at my lyre tail! Look at my lyre tail!
Lyrebird ladies, you'll like what you see!
I've the finest display on Australia's leafy forest floor.
You need my genes for your own family tree."

Next that cheeky lyrebird jumped, stepped, and bobbed his head,
He kicked his feet, lifting each lyre knee,
"With these moves, I will prove I'm the lyre guy you've been waiting for,
I'm here to wow you, come courting with me."

"Watch me, I'm dancing! Watch me, I'm dancing!
Lyrebird ladies come swing it with me!
I've the finest display on Australia's leafy forest floor.
You need my genes for your own family tree."

Many other birds don't have such fancy courtship displays. And other animals—even some spiders—can put on quite a show!

Then that noisy lyre bird cranked wide his lyre beak,
Pouring forth torrents of sound jubilee,
"Bird mimics are the bush league—I can copy *any sound I hear*—
I'm here to wow you, come courting with me."

"Listen, I'm singing! Listen, I'm singing!
Can you guess which sound I'm pretending to be?
I do birdsongs, I do car horns, human voices, even railroad trains!
You need my genes for your own family tree."

"Fabulous tail wags, fancy songs, dancing,
No other bird guy can pull off all three!
I've the finest display on Australia's leafy forest flo—
Wait! Where're you going? You *have* to pick ME!"

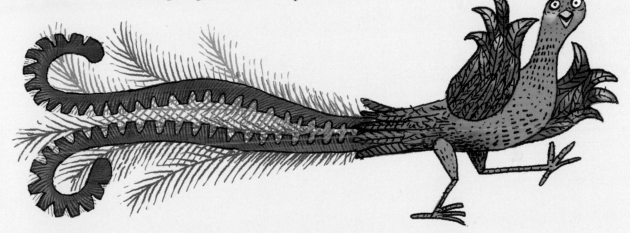

Science Note

Male birds may use dance steps, complicated songs, or fancy feathers to attract mates. But the superb lyrebird (*Menura novaehollandiae*) of southeastern Australia uses an impressive combination of all three, giving it the **fanciest courtship** display of any male bird observed.

This chicken-sized bird is also the **best mimic** of all birds, able to copy the widest range of sounds, including birdsongs, animal noises, and sounds made by people and machinery. The lyrebird get its name from its long, decorative tail, which looks a lot like an old-fashioned string instrument called a lyre.

Each male lyrebird shows off his fancy tail, sings his complex songs, and dances for a group of females from the top of a small hill of soil. The male hopes the female lyrebirds will want to mate with him. But if he's too young, or not very impressive, he will have to wait until his act improves.

Scrubfowl Parenting

This pinhead Pop with jaunty crest,
Kicks backward with his orange feet.
He builds the bird-world's biggest nest.
Mom scrubfowl's biggest job? *To eat!*

Pop kicks dead leaves with mega-feet.
His mound of litter starts to rot.
Mom kicks up seeds and snails to eat,
While rotting makes their nest grow hot.

To test their mound of forest rot,
Pop pokes his head in; Mom does, too.
When rotting litter's nicely hot,
Mom lays her eggs (as all hens do).

Pop checks and rechecks; Mom checks, too,
For proper incubation heat.
Mom buries eggs (this few birds do),
With scrubfowl mega-orange feet.

Eggs incubate in perfect heat,
Since Pop adjusts leaf-rot nonstop.
Chicks hatch, then skip on orange feet,
No scrub chitchat with Mom or Pop.

Pop tends his scrubfowl mound, nonstop,
He builds the bird world's biggest nest,
Chicks get no care from Mom or Pop—
Just pinheads with a jaunty crest!

Science Note

The orange-footed scrubfowl (*Megapodius reinwardt*) belongs to the family of ground-dwelling birds called megapodes, which means "big feet" in Greek. Many birds disguise their nests, but scrubfowl kick and pile leaf litter into the bird world's **biggest nest**. One orange-footed scrubfowl nesting mound measured 26 feet (8 meters) high and 167 feet (51 meters) across!

Both scrubfowl parents may begin the building job. But after mating, the hen forages nonstop for berries, roots, worms, and snails so she can produce giant eggs weighing one-fifth of what *she* weighs. She lays one egg every nine to twenty days (about twelve in all), burying each in a different hole in the mound.

The male keeps adding and taking away litter to be sure the work of fungi and other decomposers heat the mound to perfect incubating temperature—no egg-sitting required. Each scrubfowl chick kicks out of its eggshell with its own mega-feet. These pin-headed, jaunty-crested chicks then walk off into the forest to scratch out their own living without so much as a squawk goodbye!

Squirrels, wasps, and other animals build nests. The common murre is a seabird that lays eggs right on rocky cliffs with no nest at all!

The Great Communicator

Hop-a-dee, flit-a-dee,
small black-capped chickadee
calls out a warning most
other birds heed.

Growing or shrinking its
neuroanatomy,
sizing its song-brain
according to need!

Science Note

The black-capped chickadee (*Poecile atricapillus*) plays the role of key communicator in this collection—the same role it plays in the wild. Scientists have found that many other species of birds and some species of other animals living near chickadees can understand chickadee calls—especially warnings about predators in the area. The chickadee even gives information about how big a threat a predator might be by changing the number of *dee*'s in its warning call: *chick-a-dee-dee-dee!*

The brain is the center of a bird's neuroanatomy (nervous system). Parts of a chickadee's brain can grow or shrink during different times of the year. When it needs to remember where it is storing seeds for winter, the seed storage part of the chickadee's brain grows, and the part that learns mating songs shrinks. When a chickadee is trying to impress mates in springtime, the song-learning part of its brain grows. This brain-changing strategy saves energy. Birdbrain indeed!

For the Birds

In truth, every bird's a superlative bird,
But climate change threatens our birds. Have you heard?
One species in eight is at risk, that's the word.
The idea of Earth without birds? How absurd.

We'll keep fields and forests; birds need shrubs and trees.
We'll use plastic less—it ends up in our seas.
And pesticides, fossil fuels—*much* less of these.
Let's save our birds' futures *now*. Won't you help? Please?

Science Note

When bird habitat is altered too quickly through land-clearing, pollution, or climate change, birds may become sick or unable to reproduce. Some birds change their migration patterns and move to areas where conditions seem better. But their ecosystem jobs—like spreading seeds and pollen or controlling insect and rodent populations—may be left undone in their old habitat. And they may face new pressures such as competition, different parasites, or predation in their new areas.

Birds are remarkable, beautiful, and important, but they're also delicate. They need healthy food sources, clean air, and clean water to power flight and keep their small bodies warm. The phrase "canary in a coal mine" means that our first warnings about problems in our environment may come from studying the health of birds.

clutch—a group of eggs produced or incubated together at one time

courtship—the behaviors and interactions between a male and female of a species to signal they are ready to mate

embryo—the early developmental stages of an animal or plant before it is born, hatches, or sprouts from its seed

ferment—to convert organic food into simpler substances the body can use for energy and growth without using oxygen

forage—to search for food

hare—a fast, rabbit-like rodent with long ears and long legs

incubate—to sit or lie on eggs to warm them so they will develop and hatch

iridescent—showing shimmery colors that appear to change when viewed from different angles

krill—small relatives of shrimp that live in large swarms; an important food resource for many ocean animals, including fish, birds, and baleen whales

lemming—a chubby, short-eared, stub-tailed rodent about the size of a large hamster living in temperate and polar regions of North America, Europe, and Asia

mating—the pairing behavior in male and female animals that allows male sperm cells and female egg cells to join and create embryos

migration—the movement of a population of animals from one area to another for breeding or food supply

nectar—a sweet liquid produced by plants to attract pollinators such as birds and insects

neuroanatomy—the structures of an animal's nervous system; in vertebrates, the major neuroanatomy structure is the brain

paleontologist—a scientist who studies the evolutionary history of early life on Earth

pike—a long, pointed pole

raptor—a bird of prey

savannah—an open grassland dotted with trees and shrubs and located in a hot, dry climate

scrape—a shallow depression in the ground or in leaves, often with little or no added material, where a bird lays eggs

superlative—the highest degree of quality an adjective describes, often designated by adding "-est," as in "smelliest," or "most" as in "most numerous"

talon—the long, sharp claw on the end of the toe of a bird of prey

understory—the community of smaller shrubs and plants growing in shaded and partly shaded areas below a forest's upper canopy

vole—a mouse-sized, small-eared rodent with a tail shorter than its body

Superlative Birds

This poem introduces the big idea in this science poetry collection, namely that the poems will be about the small*est*, bigg*est*, fast*est*, fanci*est*, or otherwise *superlative* birds. The poem is arranged in four *stanzas*, or parts. The first three lines in each stanza rhyme with each other and have four STRONG beats: *WHICH birds DO what BIRDS do BEST?* The fourth line in each stanza has only three strong beats: *SuPERlative BIRDS! Come SEE!* The last line in every stanza ends with the word "see."

Less Than a Penny

Two lines that go together in a poem are called a *couplet*. This poem's two rhyming couplets are broken into very short lines to remind the reader of its subject: the tiny bee hummingbird. Short lines also encourage the reader to enjoy each word. Can you find the rhyming couplets?

A Billion Queleas

A *tendi* is a four-line stanza with Arabic origins used in traditional Swahili poetry. The first three lines rhyme with each other. Each stanza in a tendi poem ends with a *refrain*. The refrain is a repeat of the same last line in every stanza, or the same end word. Kiswahili, the language of the Swahili people, is spoken primarily in East Africa, an area where giant flocks of red-billed queleas are found.

The Flying Leap

This poem is written in *Skeltonic verse*, a form that uses short lines and lots of rhyme. The way emperor penguins zip around underwater helped me choose lines with motion. "The Flying Leap" is also a *concrete poem*, or *shape poem*.

Walk on Water

Since Spanish is the language spoken in most of the countries where the jacana lives, this poem uses a Spanish form of poetry called a *soledad*. A soledad has three lines, with eight syllables (parts of words) in each line: *The/JA/ca/NA/splays/SPIND/ly/TOES.* The first and third lines of a soledad rhyme. The poem repeats the soledad form again for a second stanza.

The Wanderer

A *limerick* is a five-line poem with two rhyme sounds and a rollicking rhythm. The first, second, and fifth lines rhyme with each other and have three strong beats in each line. The third and fourth lines rhyme and have only two strong beats. Since I added another stanza, this two-stanza poem is technically *not* a limerick.

Bird Hunter

A *tanka* is an ancient five-line poetry form from Japan. Japanese tanka poets count syllables to make lines of the following lengths: 5-7-5-7-7. Words in English have different patterns and rhythms from those in Japanese, so many tanka poets writing in English work with a tanka's shape—shorter and longer lines to allow their words to flow. The total number of syllables in an English language tanka may be fewer than the thirty-one-syllable count for a tanka written in Japanese. An interesting way to shape a tanka is to compose it so you can read lines 1, 2, 3 and lines 3, 4, 5 each as two separate haiku-like poems.

Arctic Terns the World 'Round

Song lyrics are poems, and making up new words to a song is wonderful practice with rhythm and rhyme. Since Arctic terns spend most of their lives over the sea, this poem uses the rhyme and rhythm pattern of the old *sea chantey*, "White Wings." A sea chantey is a song originating in the age of tall sailing ships (fifteenth to nineteenth centuries) that sailors sang to keep rhythm while doing a ship's repetitive physical work, such as hauling on lines (ropes) or rowing.

Crayfish for Supper

A *madsong stanza* is a five-line, funny English poetic form similar to a limerick. One exception is that the first line doesn't rhyme with any others. "Yabby" is a well-known Australian word for freshwater crayfish. This name comes from an Australian Aboriginal language—a language spoken by one of the groups of people who lived in Australia for many thousands of years before sailors from England and other cultures arrived. The Australian pelican likes to eat yabbies.

The Ghastly Pantry

A *triolet* is an eight-line poem with only two rhyme sounds. In this poem those rhymes are the *-ike* in shr*ike*, p*ike*, and str*ike*, and the long-*a* sound in aw*ay* and pr*ey*. The first and second lines are repeated as the seventh and eighth lines, and the fourth line is another repeat of the first line—so that line had better be a good one! The triolet's form—its rhyme and rhythm pattern and length—was originally developed in France, one of the many countries worldwide where shrikes are found.

Iridescent Eggs

This poem is a *kyrielle*, a French poetic form with four-line stanzas that can rhyme in couplets, or every other line. Each stanza ends in a refrain. *I/ri/DE/scent* is a word with terrific rhythm, and repeating it in the rhythmic refrain: *I/ri/DE/scent EGGS* made writing this kyrielle fun! The final refrain: *Why SIT on I/ri/DE/scent EGGS?* is a question. Scientists ask questions, then try to learn something new about possible answers.

Timberdoodle Blues

This poem is written in three-line, rhyming stanzas called *blues stanzas*. The first line in a blues stanza makes a statement that is repeated, sometimes with a little change, in the second line. The third line is a response to the first line. Blues stanzas are an American form of poetry based on African-American blues music of the 1800s. Blues music shared sorrow for life's difficulties and sometimes included a kind of humor that came from experience with—and deep understanding of—those difficulties.

Calling Contest

This poem is written in *free verse*—poetry with no rhyme or rhythm pattern. Repeated words and sounds, different line lengths, onomatopoeia (the use of words that sound like what they mean), and poem shape all can bring extra meaning and tone to a poem. Try reading the lines *the woggling ping/of the three-wattled bellbird* out loud. What sounds do you hear? Why do the last five words of the poem appear the way they do?

Barn Owl Papa

This poem is written in *cumulating* and *diminishing* verse. Cumulating means "adding to." In cumulating verse, we add a consonant to the beginning of the rhyming word at the end of each line. The word *air* at the end of the first line gains an *h* to become *hare* at the end of the second line. In the third line, *hare* gains an *s* to become *share*. The second stanza's diminishing verse "gets smaller" by losing a consonant from each line's end rhyme: *shear*, *hear*, then *ear*.

Turkey Vulture

This poem is a combination of *free verse* and *rhyme*—let's call it *free rhyme*! The poem uses rhyme without a set pattern, including rhyme within lines, as in: *Its **nose/knows** aromas*. The poem also uses end rhymes like these: *on chickeny **feet**,/and doesn't **tweet***. This loose style of rhyme mimics the rangy, but still wind-dependent flight of the turkey vulture.

What's in a Hoatzin?

This poem has six stanzas. Each stanza has three short lines. The poem could also be written in three longer stanzas, with the first stanza looking like this:

> Blunt stub beak, bald blue cheek,
> A scraggly, scrappy crest.
> Fierce red eye, hiss-grunt cry,
> Klutzy flight, at best.

Written in this form, the poem would be a *common measure* or a *ballad stanza*.

Pick Me!

More fun with music! Since the superb lyrebird lives in Australia, this poem follows the rhythm and rhyme pattern from a well-known folk song written in Australia in the late 1800s called "Waltzing Matilda."

Scrubfowl Parenting

A *pantoum* is a poem with connected stanzas. The second and fourth lines in each stanza are used to create the first and third lines in the following stanza. The lines can be exact repeats or might just use the final, rhyming word. For example, the last word in line 2 in the first stanza: *Kicks backward with his orange **feet*** is repeated in line 1 of the second stanza as: *Pop kicks dead leaves with mega-**feet***. In the pantoum's final stanza, the second and fourth lines repeat the third and first lines—or just the end words—in the very first stanza. Complicated! The pantoum form from France was based on an older poetic form called the *pantun* that many poets have used in Indonesia, a home of the orange-footed scrubfowl.

The Great Communicator

A *double dactyl* poem starts with two nonsense words. Each nonsense word is a dactyl—one word with this rhythm: *STRONG/soft/soft*. Each line of the poem has two dactyls: *HOP/a/dee, FLIT/a/dee*. The last line in each double dactyl stanza has one *STRONG/soft/soft* pattern and an additional STRONG syllable: *O/ther/birds NEED*. For an extra challenge, the second line in the second stanza should be one long word: *NEU/ro/a/NAT/o/my*, which is the scientific study of the parts of an animal's nervous system—in this case, the chickadee's brain!

For the Birds

A poet shares an idea using a small number of carefully chosen words. The idea can be a mind picture, a deep emotion, information, humor, or any combination of these elements. This poem is a call to action.

**Step outside. Find a quiet spot. Listen.
Do you hear a song in the treetops?
Are shrubs rustling?
Do you see a flicker of movement in the sky, among branches,
on the ground, or at water's edge?**

Here are a few excellent resources to help you with your birding observations:

The National Audubon Society

www.audubon.org
This information-packed portal includes bird conservation information, an online bird guide, and a hands-on "Get Outside" activities section to safely guide you from homemade feeder watches to strolls in your neighborhood, and beyond.

Cornell Lab of Ornithology

www.AllAboutBirds.org
This treasure trove for learning offers backyard birding basics, bird ID skills, exciting worldwide bird cams, online mini-courses, and much more.

Field Guide Fun!

A good take-along field guide to birds in your region such as a Peterson Field Guide, a National Audubon Society Field Guide, or a Sibley Field Guide will help you recognize and learn about the birds you will see at your feeder, in the park, or on the trail.

B is for Birders *and* Binoculars

Some local libraries have binoculars to lend. Binoculars are rugged and long-lasting, so you may also find an inexpensive used pair to buy. Audubon centers often have binoculars to lend when you join an organized bird walk, which is a terrific way to meet and learn from birders with more experience. Find nearby Audubon chapters, centers, and bird sanctuaries as well as local American Birding Association (*www.aba.org*) clubs by pairing your state, county, city, or town with either "Audubon," or "birding club" in an internet search.

Be a Superlative Citizen Scientist!

Find your local Audubon chapter and participate in the nation's largest, longest-running citizen science project, the National Audubon Society's "Christmas Bird Count." Or join Cornell's worldwide one-day bird count, the "Global Big Day," through *www.eBird.org.* Record all of your bird-watching data in a field notebook or in eBird's smartphone app, and add your data to Cornell's spectacular worldwide database. You can use the eBird database to find the superlatively birdiest parks and trails by checking eBird's regional "hotspots" maps.

black-capped
chickadee

red-billed quelea

northern jacana

bee
hummingbird

wandering albatross

peregrine falcon

emperor penguin

barn owl

salmon-crested
cockatoo

three-wattled bellbird

kakapo

On a week-long junior high field trip to Fire Island, we few early risers were treated to the rusty flash of a brown thrasher, the *"drink your teeeeee"* song of a rufous-sided (now eastern) towhee, the displaying *"conk-a-reee"* of red-winged blackbirds, and many other birding sights and sounds. Later, I spent hours at my kitchen table with guide books, colored pencils, and index cards, creating my first set of field notes: "The Birds of Fire Island." I will always be grateful to our science teacher, Mr. Soviero for sharing his passion for birding.

I try to ground each of my science poetry collections in hands-on learning experiences, so in 2015 I spent an informative and magical week at the Cornell Lab of Ornithology and its environs in Cornell's Adult University "Taking Flight" course in a congenial group of birder-learners. I'm so thankful to the "Great Scotts," Dr. Scott Taylor and Scott Haber, for their generosity and enthusiasm extending beyond class to the eventual review of this manuscript.

Many thanks to Jeff Szuc and Marc Devokaitis of Cornell's "Lab of O" for their thorough assistance with my various and sometimes obscure bird queries. One such query led to Dr. Mark Hauber, whose "eggspertise" on shell color pigments ensured an accurate portrayal of the most brilliantly colored bird eggs. Thank you, Dr. Hauber.

Interactions with scientists in the field is one of the most exciting and rewarding aspects of my work. I was lucky to have input from Dr. Julie Hagelin, Dr. Cassondra Wilson, and Dr. Jerry Kooyman, who added much appreciated insights about emperor penguins, as well as other areas of interest, including birds' sense of smell and sound production. Dr. Neils Rattenborg kindly corresponded with me about the ability of birds to "sleep on the wing" and I am grateful for his thoughtfulness and interest. I am indebted to editor Julia Robinson of the Australian National Dictionary Centre at Australian National University and her linguist colleague Dr. David Nash for information about Australian Aboriginal languages, with special thanks to Julia Robinson for the gift of the word "yabby."

My heart sings with gratitude for actor/singer/voiceover artist/daughter Julia Hirsch, who adapted and performed "Arctic Terns the World 'Round."

Finally, a sky full of thanks for the support of Peachtree Publishers, my writing buddies, and my family, and for the **most humorously accurate** imaginings of Robert Meganck; without each of you this collection could not have taken wing.

—L. B.